TOGETHER
WITH GOD

LIVING IN THE POWER
OF JESUS' GREATEST PRAYER

Larry Walkemeyer

≡XPONENTIAL˥

Together with God: Living in the Power of Jesus' Greatest Prayer
Copyright © 2020 Exponential, written by Larry Walkemeyer

Exponential is a growing movement of activists committed to the multiplication of healthy new churches. Exponential Resources spotlights actionable principles, ideas and solutions for the accelerated multiplication of healthy, reproducing faith communities. For more information, visit www.exponential.org

This book is manufactured in the United States.

Unless otherwise indicated, all Scripture quotations are taken from the Holy Bible, New International Version, copyright ©1973, 1978, 1984, 2011 by International Bible Society. All emphases in Scripture quotations have been added by the author.

Scriptures marked NLT are taken from the New Living Translation Copyright ©1996, 2004, 2007. Used by permission of Tyndale House Publishers, Inc., Carol Stream, Illinois 60188.

Scriptures marked ESV are taken from The Holy Bible, English Standard Version® (ESV®) Copyright © 2001 by Crossway, a publishing ministry of Good News Publishers. All rights reserved.

ISBN-13: 978-1-62424-052-2 (ebook)
ISBN-13: 978-1-62424-053-9 (print)

Edited by Jan Greggo

SPECIAL INVITATION

Please consider attending one of our Exponential 2020 events. Our goal is to help shape your paradigm for multiplication, inspire and encourage you to multiply, and equip you to turn ideas into action. In our 2020 conferences, we'll be focusing on what it takes to work together to pursue Kingdom collaboration.

2020 Theme: Together: Pursuing the Great Collaboration

Locations and dates: Our global conference, Exponential in Orlando, Florida, is a full-service event with thousands of attendees, 150+ speakers, 40+ tracks, and 150+ workshops. Our Exponential regional events are shorter and geographically based (translating to lower overall costs for large teams). Regionals bring the full "punch" of the national conferences' five main stage sessions without the breakout workshops.

2020 National Event
Exponential // Orlando, Florida // March 2-5, 2020

2020 Regional Events
Boise, ID// April 28-29, 2020
Exponential Español // May 1 – 2, 2020
Washington, D.C. // September 14-15, 2020
Southern California // October 7-8, 2020
Bay Area California // October 26-27, 2020
Houston // October 28-29, 2020

Chicago// November 10-11, 2020
New York City // December 2-3, 2020

Go to exponential.org/2020 to learn more.

EXPONENTIAL

MARCH 2-5, 2020
ORLANDO, FL

TOGETHER

PURSUING THE GREAT COLLABORATION

REGIONAL TOUR STOPS

Boise, ID

Exponential Español

Washington D.C.

Southern CA

Bay Area, CA

Houston, TX

Chicago, IL

New York City

JOSSY CHACKO

DAVE FERGUSON

OSCAR MURIU

DANIELLE STRICKLAND

ANDY STANLEY

SANDRA STANLEY

EFREM SMITH

PETE SCAZZERO

For more information and to register visit:

exponential.org/2020

PREFACE FROM EXPONENTIAL

Since Exponential's launch in 2006, we have come alongside church leaders to inspire, challenge and equip them to multiply disciple makers. We are a community of activists who believes that church multiplication is the best way to carry out Jesus' Great Commission and expand God's Kingdom. We dream of movements of Level 5 multipliers mobilized with new scorecards, new values, and new mindsets into every corner of society.

To help awaken that dream, Exponential is helping churches engage in the multiplication conversation through assessment tools and simple frameworks, such as the Becoming 5 framework, which has become a powerful tool churches are using throughout the world today. Other Exponential frameworks include the 3DM framework (the three critical dimensions of multiplication); five practices of hero making; the BE-DO-GO framework for mobilizing people God's way; and others (see Appendix 4 in this book for more on Exponential frameworks).

In 2020, Exponential's theme is Together: Pursuing the Great Collaboration. The framework we're introducing (and is explored in this book) says that we are called to Go (The Great Commission, Matthew 28) in Love (The Great Commandment, Mark 12) and we're called to do both Together (what we're calling The Great Collaboration, John 17).

Too many church leaders are going it alone as they start new churches instead of working together. We desperately need Level 5 leaders to emerge who will intentionally come together to catalyze movements of Level 5 multiplying churches.

If we're going to make a difference and move the multiplication needle from now 7 percent of U.S. churches ever reproducing (Level 4) to a tipping point of greater than 16 percent (resulting in tens of thousands of eternities changed), we need to start with a new scorecard and paradigm for success.

And that change must start in the heart and practices of leaders who recognize the truth that the mission of God won't be fulfilled by a few churches or dynamic leaders—but rather, hundreds of thousands of churches coming alongside each other.

You're now part of this ongoing multiplication conversation. Our prayer is that you'll learn from Larry's insights and be inspired to link arms with other leaders as together we flood the fullness of Jesus into a desperate world.

INSIDE

THE TOGETHER PRAYER

John 17

[1] *After Jesus said this, he looked toward heaven and prayed:*

*"Father, the hour has come. Glorify your
Son, that your Son may glorify you.*
[2] *For you granted him authority over all people that he
might give eternal life to all those you have given him.*
[3] *Now this is eternal life: that they know you, the only
true God, and Jesus Christ, whom you have sent.*
[4] *I have brought you glory on earth by
finishing the work you gave me to do.*
[5] *And now, Father, glorify me in your presence with
the glory I had with you before the world began.*

[6] *"I have revealed you to those whom you gave me
out of the world. They were yours; you gave them
to me and they have obeyed your word.*
[7] *Now they know that everything you
have given me comes from you.*
[8] *For I gave them the words you gave me and they
accepted them. They knew with certainty that I came
from you, and they believed that you sent me.*
[9] *I pray for them. I am not praying for the world, but
for those you have given me, for they are yours.*
[10] *All I have is yours, and all you have is mine.
And glory has come to me through them.*

¹¹ *I will remain in the world no longer, but they are still
in the world, and I am coming to you. Holy Father,
protect them by the power of your name, the name you
gave me, so that they may be ONE as we are ONE.*
¹² *While I was with them, I protected them and kept them safe
by that name you gave me. None has been lost except the one
doomed to destruction so that Scripture would be fulfilled.*

¹³ *"I am coming to you now, but I say these things
while I am still in the world, so that they may
have the full measure of my joy within them.*
¹⁴ *I have given them your word and the world has hated them,
for they are not of the world any more than I am of the world.*
¹⁵ *My prayer is not that you take them out of the world
but that you protect them from the evil one.*
¹⁶ *They are not of the world, even as I am not of it.*
¹⁷ *Sanctify them by the truth; your word is truth.*
¹⁸ *As you sent me into the world, I have
sent them into the world.*
¹⁹ *For them I sanctify myself, that they
too may be truly sanctified.*

²⁰ *"My prayer is not for them alone. I pray also for
those who will believe in me through their message,*
²¹ *that all of them may be ONE, Father, just as you
are in me and I am in you. May they also be in us so
that the world may believe that you have sent me.*
²² *I have given them the glory that you gave me,
that they may be ONE as we are ONE—*
²³ *I in them and you in me—so that they may be brought
to complete unity. Then the world will know that you sent
me and have loved them even as you have loved me.*

[24] *"Father, I want those you have given me to be with me where I am, and to see my glory, the glory you have given me because you loved me before the creation of the world.*

[25] *"Righteous Father, though the world does not know you, I know you, and they know that you have sent me.*
[26] *I have made you known to them, and will continue to make you known in order that the love you have for me may be in them and that I myself may be in them."*

(emphasis added)

INTRODUCTION

"I pray also for those who will believe in me through their message, that all of them may be ONE, Father, just as you are in me and I am in you. May they also be in us so that the world may believe that you have sent me."

– Jesus

"I have never yet known the Spirit of God to work where the Lord's people were divided."

– Dwight L. Moody

BIG IDEA: John 17 is Jesus' highest prayer for his followers and is a passionate plea for unity.

Learning and living Jesus' John 17 prayer can radically transform your life and ministry. This book explains why.

In John 17 Jesus powerfully prayed that his followers would be one with God and one another. This prayer invites us into a lifestyle of being one with the Spirit which results in being one with our brothers and sisters which produces effectiveness for the one mission we are called to. Togetherness is not just a nice idea; it has eternal implications for reaching lost people. We must become one so the world can be won by the gospel.

How do we become the answer to Jesus' prayer for the sake of the world? How do we understand and receive Jesus' prayer for us? How do we pray Jesus' prayer with him? How do we live out John 17 prayer? This book offers 10 key themes to unlock the fullness of Jesus' greatest prayer.

THE PRAYER OF COLLABORATION

Twenty-five times in the gospels we find Jesus engaged in prayer. The two most significant are, first, the prayer in Matthew 6:9-13, called "The Lord's Prayer." This most famous prayer in the world would more accurately be titled "The Disciple's Prayer" since it is the one the disciples were to learn and pray daily. It could not be our Lord's personal prayer because he had no sin to ask forgiveness for. But we need it daily.

The other momentous prayer is the John 17 prayer which is truly "The Lord's Prayer". Here Jesus prays earnestly for his current disciples, his church, and his disciples throughout the ages. This prayer is unique in all the Bible because of its length, its timing, its location, its content, its revelation, its scope and its power!

I remember a preacher pointedly asking, "What if Jesus showed up at your Bible study group, placed his hands on your shoulders and began to pray . . . what would he pray? We don't have to guess at the essence of his prayer. He would pray John 17 over you." Since then I have had a passion to let Jesus pray this over my life. My life is radically different due to this prayer.

About nine years ago, I was at a two-day retreat with nine other pastors from various denominations and independent churches in our city. We had come away together to discuss how to plant more effective churches in our city of half a million people. Eric Marsh, our leader, had us start with prayer and I couldn't get John 17 out of my mind. I kept praying phrases of it, and I finally just took out my Bible and read the entire chapter as a prayer. It was Jesus' prayer that was the reason and power of our gathering. We were there to collaborate, not for our personal brand or label, but for the sake of the gospel. Since then wonderful churches have been launched cross-denominationally in our city.

As followers of Jesus we want to see the world reached for Christ, yet we neglect collaborating together to reach it. We emphasize the great commandment - "to love God and others" and the great commission – "to go make disciples" but we have failed to understand the power of the "great collaboration" with God and others. We must come together if we want to gather in the harvest.

Collaborate comes from two Latin words which literally mean "to work" "together." Collaborate means to work jointly on an activity, especially to produce or create something.[1] In his final group prayer before the cross, Jesus lifts his gaze toward the Father and prays for a "great collaboration" between himself and his followers and between the followers themselves. He is sending them into a mission to "work jointly to create something" eternal, to collaborate. The more one they become, the closer they will co-labor together on his mission.

Praying and living this prayer will infuse you with more of the mind of Christ and the power of the Spirit than you ever imagined you could experience. These are not magic words, but they are supernatural truths meant to lead his followers forward into their destiny. The truths in this prayer will take you to new places in your life and ministry.

But warning . . . this prayer is not about you! In fact, to make it about you is to put on a blindfold while trying to view the Milky Way. It is prayer meant to be prayed and lived communally, together, in unity. It is then that the glories of heaven are revealed.

One stunning, dark summer night on a grassy hillside in Kansas, I learned a lesson in collaboration. Several of my close friends and I were laying on our backs gazing up at a brilliantly speckled star-filled sky. The sky was too big and glorious for my eyes to see. But my friends began to point things out. We saw the constellation Orion, the Milky Way, shooting stars and a satellite. Because we had viewed the night sky together, I had seen ten times more of the heavenlies than I ever had before.

The more come together, the more of God's glory we will be able to see. This is certainly a prayer that impacts "me," but far more importantly it starts with "we."

THE DIRTY FEET OF DIVISION

John 17 is one of the most lofty, yet, gritty chapters in your Bible. The entire chapter is this one prayer of Jesus that takes us into the throne room of heaven and onto the streets of our city. It reveals the priorities of Jesus for those who call themselves his followers.

An argument helped birth the greatest prayer Jesus ever prayed. Division among the team players led to Jesus' passionate intercession for unity. It was an "Every man for himself" mentality that initiated Jesus' plea to the Father that his children would be one.

The problem was dirty feet but dirtier hearts. The climactic Passover meal had been prepared featuring beans stew, olives, bitter herbs, fish sauce, lamb meat, and of course bread and wine. As the disciples entered the upper room to feast together, no servant was present to wash their feet. Consequently, they plopped themselves down on the cushions surrounding the low lying table and waited to chow down. Perhaps the odor of their unwashed feet tainted the aroma of the fresh cooked meal.

There were whispers around the table about their seating positions. There weren't assigned seats, yet their positions at the table carried significance culturally and practically. The closer they were sitting to Jesus the more prominent they felt. A "dispute" arose among them about which of them was the "greatest." Luke uses a Greek word, only employed here in scripture, *"philoneikia"* (Luke 22:24). It means a "love of strife," a "love of quarreling," or a "love of contending" as opposed to collaborating.

Philoneikia is a description of our fallen human condition. Like foot odor at a feast, it colors the air with a smell that detracts from the main focus of the meal. We love to contend for ourselves, to compare ourselves to others, to size up our position at the kingdom table. Secretly, we long to be recognized and served with attention, rather than being unknown and attending to others. Our concern is for "me" over "we." Our priority is our individuality over the community. Our secondary doctrinal positions become the identity points blocking our unity.

Depending on the size of the subject dividing us, cracks, crevices and canyons proliferate in the church. Cracks can be stepped over; crevices can be jumped over; canyons need bridges built over them to cross. Race, gender, ethics, education, economic class, political positions, nationalism, doctrinal viewpoints, church governance models, missional strategies – the list of that which separates us can be multiplied. These issues often turn into *"philoneikia."*

Jesus has a cure for *philoneikia*. Jesus is unwilling to let disputes about their personal positions disrupt this last dinner together. His remedy is a combination of example, instruction and intercession.

Jesus unobtrusively rises from the table, quietly finds the pitcher, basin and towel, then invests the next 15 minutes washing 24 unattractive feet. The lesson could not be louder - the division between them is a direct result of the selfishness within them. Jesus explains, "The example I have given you is what you should do for one another." Jesus was indicating that they were a community meant to serve one another. Their unity was paramount for the implementation of the mission. We tend to see unity in community as a Christian luxury rather than an essential which must be pursued with intentionality.

THE POWER OF *UBUNTU*

Dr. Dennis Kilama of Africa Renewal University exhorts the church towards unity by explaining that *Ubuntu* is an African philosophy that, when redeemed by the gospel, can serve the church well. *Ubuntu* says people exist in community not isolation. We are human because of our interconnectedness with other humans. *Ubuntu* is a word used by several Bantu tribes in East and Southern Africa to depict "humanness." It is a word that is difficult to translate into English. It is an attitude of faithfulness and commitment to the group, above success of the individual.[2]

Our churches have become places where the focus is helping individuals thrive and prosper. The community is only useful if it serves the goals of the individual. *Ubuntu* flips that. *Ubuntu* says that when our goal is to help the community, the byproduct is the individual fulfillment we seek.

God as a community of the Trinity created us to live in unity with one another (Genesis 1-2). The fall opened the door to division (Genesis 3) with the first murder occurring in Genesis 4. God's answer is foreshadowed in Genesis 12 when a new community of his people is promised. John 17 is a prayer for the fulfillment of that community upon earth; for *Ubuntu* to spread through God's people.

When we refuse the individualism of our fallenness and of our Western culture and practice the foot-washing community of the Jesus culture, we position ourselves for God's best blessings.

John 17 is best read with Psalm 133 serving as a beautiful backdrop of promise.

Psalm 133
How good and pleasant it is
when God's people live together in unity!
It is like precious oil poured on the head,
running down on the beard,
running down on Aaron's beard,
down on the collar of his robe.
It is as if the dew of Hermon
were falling on Mount Zion.
For there the Lord bestows his blessing,
even life forevermore.

The anointing we long for personally, the anointing our ministries desperately need, is available, but it awaits this "togetherness," this "oneness," this "unity" Jesus prays for in John 17. When God sees his people pursuing unity with himself and others, it's like a magnet to his heart. He takes his most expensive oil and begins to drench his people with his blessing. It flows over our head, our face, our neck. It is like the heavy dew of Mount Hermon which waters the meadows to produce both flowers and trees. Unity is the place of abundant blessing.

It is sadly surprising that so few Christians ever stop to deeply examine the most important prayer Jesus ever prayed. We speak in broad generalities about unity without understanding from whence this unity arises, what elements constitute this unity, and what this unity can accomplish. Over the next chapters we will taste the dynamic truth of 10 of the key words or concepts Jesus uses in his high priestly prayer. We will see what Jesus is praying for us in John 17 and how this can revolutionize our lives. We will discover how to become the answer to Jesus' "one" prayer.

CHAPTER TAKEAWAYS:

- Collaboration is the means of seeing more of God and doing more for God.
- Our self-focus is the key disruptor to the unity Jesus prays for.
- The priority on community above individualism is central to being the answer to Jesus' prayer.

I see the importance of the local church working together as one. Every member doing their part for the good of all. But, on a high level I see the universal church working together + unified + the local church being like 'small groups' of that unity.

CHAPTER 1
Together in Prayer

*John 17:1 "After Jesus said this, he looked
toward heaven and prayed:"*

"The Church has to come together on its knees."
– Charles Colson

BIG IDEA: Prayer is God's primary tool for building togetherness in the body of Christ.

It has been stated, "If you want to divide the church, have a board meeting; if you want to unite the church, hold a prayer meeting." Jesus didn't end his final teaching dinner with a strategy session or a vision-casting rally. He "looked toward heaven" and prayed. He wrapped his words in the power of prayer. He punctuated his revelation with intercession.

Jesus' formal ministry began with forty days of fasting and prayer. It finished with dinner and prayer. John 17 is by far his longest recorded prayer. His petition to his Father is built on a lifetime of conversation but this plea is an especially earnest one.

His themes of glory, protection, indwelling, sanctification, mobilization, and unity are so priceless that it is not enough to simply preach them to his disciples, they must be prayed into them. Jesus' desire is not merely to teach these holy truths but to impart the example of intercessory prayer on behalf of these truths.

If Jesus prayed for these spiritual realities to be manifest, then we, too, must not just believe them, or practice them, but also pray them. If Jesus deemed these John 17 subjects worthy of intense prayer, then surely we should be joining him in praying for the same thing in the same way. How earnestly do we join Jesus in praying for what he prays for in John 17?

PRAYER IS BEST WHEN DONE WITH OTHERS

Jesus has a prayer that he will pray alone in the garden. It is a prayer that three of his friends can get close to, but do not enter into. Soon he will take the eleven to the garden, the three deeper into the garden, and then will continue on "a stone's throw" away to pour out his heart one on one to the Father (Luke 22:41).

But this John 17 prayer is not a prayer for solitude. It is a communal prayer, prayed to bring his Father and his followers together as one. He may have prayed it slowly or repeated each petition several times to allow them to penetrate the depths of his friend's heart. We know John's mind was captured by it, as years later he recalled (with the Spirit's assistance) the exact phrases Jesus lifted up.

I don't know about you, but my Mama taught me to pray with my eyes shut and my head bowed. I was to shut my eyes to focus on my own heart and not the world around me. I bowed my head to show reverence and so I wouldn't look at the people around me praying. Did Mama teach me wrong? My sister followed her instructions religiously. Me? Not so much. It's why my sister would occasionally find chewing gum in her hair when prayer time was finished.

Here Jesus positions himself with his eyes open and his head lifted toward heaven. He is focused on the Father, but he can still see everyone in the room. Even when we lead in prayer we often have a tendency to isolate ourselves from the others present. Prayer is community property meant to be a shared moment to release its uniting power.

It seems that the church in America has not made the word "our" inclusive enough. Let me explain. When the disciples requested that Jesus would teach them to pray in the unique way that he prayed, Jesus instructed them in a patterned prayer. The first word of this prayer was, "Our," setting the tone and target for the rest of the prayer. "Our" is used four times in the prayer and "us" is used twice. Jesus wanted to teach a form of prayer that was communal, not individualistic, that was embracive, not separatist. This is why our prayers must begin with "Our" and be wide enough to include all those who have "God as Father" because they have "Jesus as Savior."

Prayer was Jesus' means to initiate a movement. The next day, the cross would give substance to the life-altering truths of this new gospel movement. But in this last "all group" moment, Jesus engages in the act of prayer. Prayer was the initial and final response he desired for his disciples to practice upon his departure.

PRAYER BRIDGES THE GAPS BETWEEN US

Jesus knew he, the good shepherd, would be struck and the "sheep would be scattered" (Zechariah 13:7) by the events which would transpire over the next several hours. So Jesus earnestly prays for them to be reunited as one to give witness to the world. Jesus hands his disciples the gift of this special prayer for them and for all their spiritual lineage. Jesus believed the power of prayer could reach down through the days, decades, centuries and millennium to call back together those whom the evil one would scatter.

For the church of the 21st century to have the impact of the church in the 1st century, we must reprioritize prayer to give it the same place Jesus and the disciples did. The church today continues to want supernatural results with natural methods. We say we believe in the power of prayer, but our actions show a far greater reliance upon our own talents, creativity, persuasion, oratory skills, charisma, ambiance, coolness and vibe.

Prayer has the ability to change the atmosphere and unify the one invisible church in a city or region. The disunity of the church is largely due to the fact we spend so little time in prayer together. If we would join in prayer for the themes Jesus prayed for in John 17, we would be surprised at the results.

For the past year and a half, I have hosted a monthly National Church Planters Prayer Gathering on behalf of Exponential. People from across the nation and around the world join together with no agenda except to pray for the themes Jesus prayed for in John 17. Four national leaders from various denominations and networks are recruited and agree to help lead these prayer times. Usually the four leaders do not know each other prior to this time of prayer. Often, they come from divergent streams in the body of Christ, even holding contrary doctrinal positions on several subjects. Yet, as we begin and proceed to pray together, something supernatural transpires. There is a spiritual unity which begins to infuse these new relationships. It is difficult to sincerely pray for the lost, for evangelism, for holiness, for the church without starting to come together.

Remember the disciples were only two or three hours past John 13, where they were asserting their own positions of honor and contending with one another. Now in John 17, Jesus is holding a prayer meeting, leading them into the Father's presence with a division-bridging time of intercession. Don't miss this: His remedy for disunity is a prayer meeting.

UNITED PRAYER UNLEASHES UNUSUAL GOSPEL MOVEMENT

Jesus knows the power of an earnest prayer gathering. Indeed, it is the next upper room prayer gathering when the scattered disciples are again "all together in one place" that the Holy Spirit is poured out and the first gospel movement kicks off in high gear (Acts 1,2).

Even a slow student of church history will quickly discover that awakenings of the church and gospel movements down through the centuries have almost without exception started with prayer. It is prayer that propels believers over the walls of division of denominationalism, sexism, racism, classism to kneel side by side before God's throne and travail for revival.

On September 23, 1857, Jeremiah Lanphier, a middle-aged businessman in New York, but more importantly a man of prayer, announced a prayer meeting at noon. It was to be held in a small room on the third floor of an old church on Fulton Street. On the day of the meeting, Lanphier climbed the stairs, began to pray and wait and no one showed . . . until 12:30pm. Then one by one, six individuals he had never met, joined him. One was a Baptist, one a Congregationalist, one a Dutch Reformed member, one a Presbyterian, but those differences were forgotten as these men began to pray.

As they united in prayer, God answered in an unusual manner. The next week, twenty even more diverse pray-ers were there. The next Wednesday, forty were interceding. The meetings were moved from weekly to daily. The numbers grew exponentially. Lawyers were praying next to messenger boys. People from all denominations were joining together. Conversions were happening at a rapid pace. Within six months, 10,000 people in New York were gathered for prayer at noon. The revival spread to other cities. Estimates are that as many as a million people came to saving faith during 1857 and 1858.[3]

1800 years earlier a diverse group of believers set themselves to fast and pray for God's movement. The setting was the young church at Antioch. Leaders in the church included Barnabas, a Jew from Cyprus; Lucius from Cyrene in North Africa; Simeon who was also a Jew but also went by the name of Niger, (a Roman name indicating involvement in Roman circles); Manaen who was a man with aristocratic connections; and Paul, a famous rabbi from Tarsus in Cilicia. This was a multi-cultural and multi-class church staff! But this dissimilar group of leaders had been joined in Jesus and were now giving themselves to united prayer. What happened?

"While they were worshiping the Lord and fasting, the Holy Spirit said, "Set apart for me Barnabas and Saul for the work to which I have called them." So after they had fasted and prayed, they placed their hands on them and sent them off." (Acts 13:2,3) A movement was launched. The first recorded church planting sending took place. A mission which would dramatically multiply the fledgling church of Jesus was launched in response to a diverse group agreeing together in prayer.

The church I pastor has only 39 parking spots and had grown to 800 in attendance in 1999. We were ready to move and hopefully become really big. But God first called us to forty days of fasting and prayer. During that time God brought our diverse multi-ethnic church together in unity to stay in the neighborhood and become a "river" church where people would flow in, be equipped then flow out in church planting. What happened? A small movement was started. Today many thousands in America and around the world worship in churches birthed by the earnest, united prayers of the saints.

The same principle at work in Antioch is available today. The power of uniting in prayer to unite the church and propel multiplication of the church is a virtually untapped resource. Yet, Jesus modeled this tool and prayed that his church would be made ONE so the world would be won. We have the opportunity to be the answer to Jesus' prayer . . . but only if we come together in prayer.

CHAPTER TAKEAWAYS:

- Jesus' prayer was a communal prayer inviting us to pray in community as well.
- Prayer is God's primary means of bridging the gaps in the body of Christ.
- Prayer is the key means to initiate Gospel movements.

CHAPTER 2

Together in the Glory

John 17:1 "Glorify your Son, that your Son may glorify you"

17:4,5 "I have brought you glory on earth by finishing the work you gave me to do. And now, Father, glorify me in your presence with the glory I had with you before the world began."

17:10b " . . . And glory has come to me through them."

17:22 "I have given them the glory that you gave me, that they may be one as we are one—"

17:24 "Father, I want those you have given me to be with me where I am, and to see my glory, the glory you have given me because you loved me before the creation of the world."

"If you had a thousand crowns you should put them all on the head of Christ! And if you had a thousand tongues they should all sing his praise, for he is worthy!"
– William Tiptaft

BIG IDEA: Focusing on God's glory brings us together with God and others.

Unity is built when we live fully focused on ONE glory – God's!

TOUCHING THE MEANING OF GLORY

Jesus saturates his final group prayer with the theme of glory. The word, *glory* or its variations, are used eight times in this prayer. While *glory* is a difficult term for our human minds to comprehend, we must lean hard into the soaring majesty of the truth of glory.

This word *glory* can be confusing since it is used in a variety of ways. For example, Jesus said, "Glorify your Son" (v. 2); "I have glorified You on earth" (v. 4); "I have been glorified in them" (v. 10); "they will see My glory" (v. 24). Sometimes it is used as a noun, other times as a verb. The basic idea of *glory* in the Hebrew is "weightiness." Something that has *glory* has such significance, power, transcendence that it is "heavy with importance." It has a majestic brilliance or shininess due to its radiant splendor and essential dignity. *Glory* is defined by who God is since God is by far the weightiest reality.

Gold is sold by the ounce. Diamonds are measured and valued by the carats. The heavier the weight, the more valuable the substance. If a global-size scale could be devised and the wealth and power of the world were placed on one side and God could be placed on the other, it would be like a feather had been compared to an elephant. God is heavy with glory. He is the fundamental definition of glory. He "has" glory but also "is" glory.

To glorify God is to recognize, revere, revel in, and proclaim the essential nature of his "Godness." We announce His worth, beauty, value, power, wisdom, compassion and exclusivity to ourselves and all others. To "give glory to" is "to bring admirable attention to."

STOPPING THE GLORY GRABBERS

Have you been around "glory grabbers?" You know the people who want the attention and admiration given to themselves. These are the name droppers, the talkers who give compliments to others only in order to bring the spotlight back to themselves, the back slappers who are really patting their own backs. They give God the credit if doing so brings more glory to themselves. They are experts at the "humble brag" on social media. They want to tell you how good God is as long as their face is in the picture . . . it's celebrate Jesus . . . and me! "Glory grabbers" are not only ultimately hurting themselves, they are hindering the oneness of the church and slowing her advance.

Jesus' was the opposite of a "glory grabber." His one purpose is stated in his opening prayer request – "Glorify your Son, that your Son may glorify you." You must read this request in light of his preceding statement in his prayer, "Father, the hour has come." What hour is Jesus speaking of? The hour he was born for. The hour of ultimate sacrifice for the sin of humanity. The hour of the cross. The hour of total humiliation which would simultaneously bring the hour of his glory as he fully obeys his Father's will.

Jesus' one purpose was to glorify his Father, even at the price of his own life. But this one determination had been manifested all through his life. In his John 17 prayer he goes on to declare, "I have brought you glory on earth by finishing the work you gave me to do (John 17:4).

Although the cross was "the hour" he had been born for, every hour of his life had pointed toward this pivotal hour. His life was lived for the work the Father had given him to do. Every hour had been for the glory of God. He did his assigned work to bring admiration to his Father.

Is this our determination? Is our passion to bring attention, affection and admiration to our Father? Or do we want to be applauded for own sake? Or do we wish we had someone else's ministry story? We would get much further in our race if we stopped trying to run in other people's lanes. Stay in your lane for the glory of God and you will finish your appointed work. Also, you will contribute to, rather than detract from, the unity God desires in his body.

THE UNIFYING POWER OF GLORY SHARING

In John 17:22 you are met with an even greater mystery - Jesus says, "I have given them the glory that you gave me, that they may be one as we are one—" (John 17:22).

The brand of glory shared among the Godhead is shared with us! We are included in this glory. Jesus shares his own glory with us who are born of His Spirit. This glory is given to unify us like Jesus and the Father.

The unity Jesus is imparting here is a distinct brand of "oneness". It is not a oneness that the world can produce through philosophical alignments, emotional harmony, or political agreements. It is not like the unity is a great sports team.

No, this is a oneness created by the Spirit in the same manner as is experienced in the Godhead. As such, we can't attain it through our wisdom or effort. This is a supernatural gift that has a practical incarnation in our relationships. This manifestation is a passion and practice of giving glory to one another and not to ourselves. We follow the triune God's example of honoring one another as we honor other believers because they too are carriers of the Spirit. We glorify Christ in them.

God really meant it when he said in Isaiah 42:8 "I am the LORD; that is my name! I will not give my glory to anyone else . . . " He shares his glory with his children, but it's not a giving away of glory. Ours is a "derived glory." It is a glory which is sourced only from Him; we only share in what still belongs to him. Our glory is secondary glory arising from his primary glory. This is why to take any of his glory for ourselves becomes a treacherous act inducing a significant break in the church's unity. We can't be ONE if we are hijacking God's glory for ourselves.

How well do we share in God's glory by bringing glory to the Christ in one another?

Jesus prayed something for us that I am anticipating with a childlike wonder and impatience. I know since Jesus prayed it, it will be fully answered. What was it?

Towards the end of his prayer Jesus makes this unique request in John 17:24, "Father, I want those you have given me to be with me where I am, and to see my glory, the glory you have given me because you loved me before the creation of the world."

Jesus yearns for his disciples to bask in the unmasked glory of his full Lordship . . . like the Mount of Transfiguration on steroids. This is not some ego-driven last request. It is a desire for a different brand of foot-washing. To serve his friends with the overwhelming joy and thrilling splendor of his loving triune presence with absolutely no filters. Can you even imagine such a glory?

Have you ever seen something so awesome, so magnificent that your first thought was I wish _____ (fill in the blank with the name of someone you love) could be here to see this?

When I saw the Northern Lights for the first time I had to just shout aloud, "Wow! God! Wow! You are just, Wow! Glory to you God!" But my next thought was, "I wish (about 20 names came to mind) could see this! This is what it means to be one, to collaborate, to sincerely love Christ's church. It is to see such a splendid glory that your desire is not to consume it but to share it . . . to not enter into it unless you can bring others with you!

Soon we will live in perfect unity and in the fullness of His glory. John described the New Jerusalem we are headed for in this way: "The city does not need the sun or the moon to shine on it, for the **glory** of God gives it light, and the Lamb is its lamp" (Revelation 21:23). That, my friend, is the ultimate fulfillment of Jesus' John 17 prayer.

CHAPTER TAKEAWAYS:

- Glory is central to living together with God and bringing people together for God.
- Grabbing the glory for ourselves diminishes unity with God and others.
- Sharing in God's glory means we see his glory in one another.

CHAPTER 3

Together in the Truth

John 17:6 "I have revealed you to those whom you gave me out of the world. They were yours; you gave them to me and they have obeyed your word."

17:8 "For I gave them the words you gave me and they accepted them."

17:14 "I have given them your word and the world has hated them, for they are not of the world any more than I am of the world."

17:17 "Sanctify them by the truth; your word is truth."

"The Bible is the inevitable outcome of God's continuous speech. It is the infallible declaration of His mind."

– A.W. Tozer

BIG IDEA: An increasing love for God's truth is the only infallible path to unity.

USING THE BIBLE AS A MAP

We are brought together with God and one another by knowing and living the one book.

Individuals starting from very different points can end up the same place if they use the same map. A true map depicts reality.

It defines the roads which much be taken to reach a certain destination.

When Jesus was uttering his final group prayer he was lifting up the map which would lead to unity. Jesus turns three times to this phrase, "your word" and once to "the words you gave me." God's word is what he has given them (17:8,14), God's word is what they have obeyed (17:6), God's word is what will sanctify them (17:17), God's word is the definer of all that can rightly be called truth (17:17).

Jesus, knowing of his departure the following day, turns the attention of his friends to the authority which will be there when he is gone. Jesus prays for them and us that we would know the Word, obey the Word, be changed by the Word, and filter all thoughts through the Word. Using God's word correctly would bring about the togetherness Jesus was praying for.

"Homo unius libri" - these are the words that John Wesley used to describe himself. They are words Jesus prayed for every believer in John 17. "Home unius libri" – A man of one book. The Bible was his one book. Yet, Wesley owned over 1,000 books, ranging from Christian history to medicine, politics, poetry, and beyond.[4] Wesley was a life-long reader of many books. Yet, the Bible was Wesley's truth source. Every other book was read in the light of the one book.

It was this passion for the one book that would prompt Wesley to say, "I want the whole Christ for my Savior, the whole Bible for my book, the whole Church for my fellowship and the whole world for my mission field." When the Bible is truly our one book it will create a desire for "the whole church to be our fellowship!"

DISTINGUISHING THE DIFFERENCES THAT MAKE A DIFFERENCE

Yet, the opposite is so often the case. Most Christian division is doctrinal in nature. It is the variety of interpretations we arrive at from the one book that causes suspicion and separation in the one church. Our doctrinal differences become our relational distances.

Whether "the Word" unifies or divides depends on how we use the Word. If we use it as a point of agreement on the primary doctrines, it unifies us. If we use it to humble us and sanctify our attitudes towards ourselves and others, it unifies us.

N.T. Wright gets it right when he states, "We have to tell the difference between the differences that make a difference, and the differences that don't make a difference."[5] When we major in our differences that make no difference, we divide the body of Christ.

The definitive and classic quote in this regard is - "In essentials unity, in non-essentials liberty, in all things charity." Philip Schaff, the distinguished nineteenth-century church historian, calls the saying, "the watchword of Christian peacemakers" (*History of the Christian Church*, vol. 7, p. 650). Often attributed to great theologians such as Augustine, it comes from an otherwise undistinguished German Lutheran theologian of the early 17th century, Rupertus Meldenius. The phrase occurs in a tract on Christian unity written (circa 1627) during the Thirty Years War (1618–1648), a bloody time in European history in which religious tensions played a significant role.[6]

Meldenius' quote is an excellent posture to take to promote Christian unity. Of course, for the thinking person it quickly prompts the question, *"Which truths are essential, and which are non-essential?"* Does the Bible itself imply a difference between essential and non-essential teachings of scripture? Scripture would answer with a definitive "yes" and Jesus would encourage to discern the difference.

Jesus tells the teachers of the law that some matters in the law are weightier than others, some are gnats and some are camels (Matthew 23:24,25).

In 1 Corinthians 15:3 Paul uses the term, "first importance." He applies this to the sacrificial death, burial and resurrection of Christ.

These are truths of "first importance" implying that indeed, there were truths of secondary importance.

Paul distinguishes between foundation and what is built *on* the foundation. The foundation is Christ himself, and there is no building without that foundation, it is essential. What is built *on* that foundation may differ. Some of the building blocks placed on that foundation may be gold and silver, others may be wood and hay. Though important, the building blocks are not the same value as the foundation. (1 Corinthians 3:11-13)

Romans 14 speaks to this matter when Paul takes on a difference of opinion within the Roman church. Romans 14:5 says, "One person considers one day more sacred than another; another considers every day alike. Each of them should be fully convinced in their own mind." Paul could have handed down an apostolic declaration of truth. Instead he seems more interested in teaching them tolerance for contrasting views on non-essential doctrines.

Recently, the Evangelical Free Church of America voted to drop "premillennial" from their statement of faith. "The thought was, we must either stop saying we are a denomination that majors on the majors . . . and minors on the minors, or we must stop requiring premillennialism as the one and only eschatological position," said Greg Strand, EFCA executive director of theology.[7] This type of irenic thinking helps us toward unity in the body of Christ.

I have been aided in my own views through a model presented in an article by theological professor and author, Keith Drury. Drury writes of his own developmental journey in regard to the essentials and non-essentials. Along the way he discovers that many doctrines or practices are written in pencil, some in pen and a few in blood.[8]

The pencil items are those which are tertiary in their relative importance. They are more easily erased or changed. The doctrines written in ink are more important, of greater weight and must be written over, not just erased. These are doctrines which tend to group evangelical denominations together in the same general camps.

The truths written in blood are those which are a matter of life and death for the church. They capture the irreducible minimums of our biblical positions which bring us into union with Christ.

They are the lifeblood of all Christians everywhere. These are few, weighty, unchangeable and agreed upon by all true Christians because without them, something of critical essence is lost.

LETTING LOVE FRAME DOCTRINAL DISCUSSIONS

The more the church focuses on those "blood" truths the more unified we become. Our pencil and even our pen marks will not all agree until Jesus returns. Therefore, Paul's words in 1 Corinthians 8:1b-2 become paramount – " . . . knowledge puffs up while love builds up. Those who think they know something do not yet know as they ought to know."

Whenever you are debating a theological point but are more concerned with winning the argument than loving your neighbor, you have already lost on Jesus' scoreboard. Those who pride themselves in scripture knowledge must prioritize the unmistakable teaching of scripture to be gentle, kind, patient, merciful, peaceful, gracious, encouraging, etc. The application of those clear teachings will create the context for how we carry and discuss those more debatable doctrines.

Church history brings us one of the most poignant examples of this. John Wesley and George Whitfield go down as two of the most influential leaders in Christian history. They were close friends who disagreed on one important doctrine. Whitfield was a stringent Calvinist and Wesley was an ardent Arminian. Yet they refused to allow it to destroy their friendship and admiration for one another. So much so that at Whitfield's request, John Wesley gave Whitfield's funeral sermon. It was during that sermon that a well-known and vital phrase was first put into print – "We may agree to disagree." The expanded quote from Wesley's sermon says, "There are many doctrines of a less essential nature . . . In these we may think and let think; we may 'agree to disagree.' But meantime, let us hold fast the essentials . . . "[9] Whitfield and Wesley were brothers, who worked together to see people won for Christ.

Being people of "one book" is God's path for us to come together with himself and others.

CHAPTER TAKEAWAYS:

- Using God's truth as a map towards Christian unity is an answer to Jesus' prayer.
- Distinguishing and prioritizing the essential truths of scripture is a key to unity.
- Pursuing love as the frame for all our doctrinal discussions is essential.

CHAPTER 4

Together in His Name

17:11, 12 "I will remain in the world no longer, but they are still in the world, and I am coming to you. Holy Father, protect them by the power of your name, the name you gave me, so that they may be one as we are one. While I was with them, I protected them and kept them safe by that name you gave me."

"To holy people the very name of Jesus is a name to feed upon, a name to transport. His name can raise the dead and transfigure and beautify the living."

— John Henry Newman

BIG IDEA: Jesus gave us his name to unify us and protect us.

The more passionate we are to live under the protection and for the proclamation of the one name, the more unified we will be. The more we elevate the name of Jesus, the more we will collaborate for the mission of Jesus.

Three times in his John 17 prayer, Jesus uses the word, "name." Each time he ties his name back to his Father – John 17:11 - "your name," "the name you gave me;" John 17:12 - "by the name you gave me." Jesus underlines his unity with the Father by saying, "I bear your name and you gave it to me"."

Jesus is praying that his followers would live in his name, by the power of his name, under the protection of his name, being unified by his name. Jesus says, *Father, I am coming to you and leaving them here but I am leaving them what they need – the power of your name!* This is central to Jesus' prayer that his disciples would be one. Jesus links his name to their unity – "protect them by the power of your name, the name you gave me, SO THAT they may be one."

The church and her leaders are too often living in the power of their own names and the result is a disunified church and discordant message to the world.

In 1995 I was in the press box of the Los Angeles Coliseum gazing down on 55,000 men who had come together for the Promise Keeper's rally. One of the speakers had the men participate in a moment that is etched deep in my memory banks. He directed them on the count of three to shout their names. As they did it was unintelligible cacophony of sound. After they quieted down the speaker said, "Now on the count of three scream the name of your church". The result was an even greater release of audio chaos. He then exclaimed, "Now on three, as loud as you can, shout the name of your Savior and Lord!" When "three" hit, the name of Jesus filled the stadium as if one voice made up of 55,000 tongues was released into the atmosphere. "JESUS!" The unity, power and glory were so thick you could feel it on your skin.

The preacher could have sat down at that point because his point was made: The more we are unified around the name of Jesus, the more powerful our witness will be. That moment has given me a glimpse of the fulfillment of Jesus' John 17 prayer and a vision for what the church can develop into.

One of Jesus' best promises is, "For where two or three gather in my name, there am I with them" (Matthew 18:20). This is the church unified at its most simple level. When we gather in union with his name, his presence is released in a magnified manner. His name, not as some label, but as a foundation and centerpoint, brings people together in a way nothing else can.

JESUS THE PERSON, NOT JUST THE NAME

Naming a child can feel like an ominous responsibility. Mary and Joseph didn't face that "naming" pressure. The Father was so protective about the naming of the child, he sent supernatural revelation to both Joseph and Mary individually. Gabriel announces to Mary in Luke 1:31, "Behold, you will conceive and give birth to a son, and you are to give Him the name Jesus." Then another angel pays a middle of the night house call to Joseph in Matthew 1:21 and says, "she will give birth to a Son, and you shall give Him the name Jesus, because He will save His people from their sins."

God the Father gave the name to his Son and Jesus declared this fact throughout his ministry and especially in this John 17 prayer. Names in Biblical times often carried the character and/ or the mission of the person being named. This fact is in view in Matthew 1:21 when the angel gives the underlying rationale for the name "Jesus" – "because He will save His people from their sins."

Jesus fulfilled his name through his life, death and resurrection. He saved "his people from their sins" and "his people" became those who carried his name. All Christians are "Jesus people."

When we are born, we are named by our parents; when we are born again, we are named by our God. We bear his name on our hearts. But eventually that name will be tattooed on our foreheads (at least symbolically). In the last chapter of the Bible we have a promise: "They will see his face, and his name will be on their foreheads" (Revelation 22:4).

The name that saved us, the name that protects us, the name that is the message of our lives, the name that every knee will bow to, the name which we will wear for eternity – that name should unite us now. IF it is lifted high above our own names, our church names, our denominational names, it will bring us together. Jesus made it clear: " . . . protect them by the power of your name, the name you gave me, <u>so that</u> they may be one as we are one" (John 17:11).

JESUS IS NOT A MAGIC WORD

There are three primary challenges to our unity as it relates to the name of Jesus. The first is people who are using the name as a magic word without seeking genuine relationship to the one who carries the name. Although there are many variations of this disassociation, one vivid example happens in Acts 19.

In Acts 19 a Jewish chief priest, named Sceva had seven sons who became a traveling ministry team. These magnificent seven confronted a demon-possessed man and they use the latest spiritual power they had heard about . . . the name of Jesus. In a loose paraphrase the demon retorts, "Believe me I know Jesus, and I know about Paul who is a Jesus carrier, but who in the heck are you?" Then one demon gives a whipping to these seven wannabe exorcists.

The problem was clear, they used the name of Jesus without connection to Jesus. But notice what happens next as described in Acts 19:17, "When this became known to the Jews and Greeks living in Ephesus, they were all seized with fear, and the name of the Lord Jesus was held in high honor." The diverse population of Ephesus began to come together in revival because the name of Jesus is exalted.

Before we too quickly write off such behavior as non-applicable to ourselves, we need to ask if we ever use the name of Jesus as our abracadabra. When we fill our shopping cart of prayer with selfish desires then pronounce the magic words, "in Jesus name" over them, we are doing something similar to the antics of the boys of Sceva.

The second challenge is those who want to be called by the name of Jesus but aren't interested in the character of Jesus. They desire the label of Jesus without the lifestyle of Jesus. They are using the name of Jesus as their ticket to heaven but not making him their teacher for life. To take the name of Jesus for ourselves means we want to be like Jesus. (More on this later.)

PLAYING FOR THE NAME ON THE FRONT

A third challenge is those who want to leverage the name Jesus to build the notoriety of their own name. These are the ones Paul speaks of in his letter to the Philippian believers – "It is true that some preach Christ out of envy and rivalry, but others out of goodwill . . . . The former preach Christ out of selfish ambition, not sincerely, supposing that they can stir up trouble for me while I am in chains" (Philippians 1:15,17). The motives of envy, rivalry and selfish ambition drive far too much ministry today. Such motives divide the team and hinder the mission of the church.

Ball hogs are the bane of NBA teams. A "ball hog" is a player who seems more concerned about their player stats than their teams wins and losses. In most professional sports, players wear jerseys with their team names on the front and their own name on the back. This has given rise to a popular and quite true saying: "Play for the name on the front of the jersey, not the one on the back." The more the Jesus team can follow this advice the more unified we will be.

The name of Jesus is the banner that brings the church together as one. It bridges across every divide of language, nation, culture, class, denomination, education. Having traveled the world in ministry efforts, I am always amazed at how unifying the name of Jesus is.

But the word, *Jesus* as a word is no different than any other word. In fact, many Jewish boys were named Jesus when our Jesus was born in Bethlehem. It was as common as John is in our culture today. The first century Jewish historian, Josephus, mentions at least 12 different people he knew with the name, Jesus, including four High Priests.[10]

The name of our Jesus, THE Jesus, carries power because it is the one-word summary of all who this one person is. The power in the name is the person behind the name and that person brings us together when we play for His name alone.

CHAPTER TAKEAWAYS:

- Jesus emphasized the importance of being carriers of His name.
- There is power in the name of Jesus when we use it in connection to Jesus himself.
- Investing our lives to promote the name of Jesus unites us with others doing the same.

CHAPTER 5

Together Against the Evil One

17:11,12 "I will remain in the world no longer, but they are still in the world, and I am coming to you. Holy Father, protect them by the power of your name, the name you gave me, so that they may be one as we are one. While I was with them, I protected them and kept them safe by that name you gave me . . . "

17:14,15 "I have given them your word and the world has hated them, for they are not of the world any more than I am of the world. My prayer is not that you take them out of the world but that you protect them from the evil one."

"I could well believe that it is God's intention, since we have refused milder remedies, to compel [Christians] into unity, by persecution even. Satan is without doubt nothing else than a hammer in the hand of a benevolent and severe God."

– C.S. Lewis

BIG IDEA: God uses our enemy to unite us if we choose togetherness. Independence kills.

PRAYING AGAINST THE LIONS

My aunt and uncle were missionaries in Africa in an area where lions were active. As a young boy of five we visited them for a few weeks one summer. I remember walking to an area where they were beginning a new ministry. At times you could hear lions roar. I was frightened, but my uncle reassured me with these words – "We will be safe if we walk together."

Many Christians fail to realize that Jesus takes our protection so seriously that he commands us to pray about it daily. When Jesus answered his disciple's request to teach them how to pray, he offered a model prayer and says, "This, then, is how you should pray" (Matthew 6:9).

In this prayer, Jesus exhorts us to pray, "And deliver us from evil" (Matthew 6:13). Many translations render this "And deliver us from the evil one" I believe both are in view. We need deliverance from all "evil" flowing from "the evil one." What is often missed here, however, is the two-letter word "us." Jesus wanted us to pray for protection for and with other brothers and sisters. Our deliverance is found in the power of unity, especially unity in prayer.

If we dare to prioritize great collaboration, the devil will resist it with his mightiest weapons. Christians united and laboring together on mission are the biggest threat to Satan's plan to stop the evangelism of the world.

When we read Jesus' John 17 prayer, he is not asking the Father to keep his disciples from danger, but to protect them as they minister in treacherous territory. A key to that safety is walking together, united under the power of His name. Our unity will be a key to our security. Independence may get you killed. Division is one of the devil's primary weapons against the gospel.

CONFRONTING THE CULTURE OF DIVISION AND INDIVIDUALISM

Every Christian has powerful enemies. The realities of these enemies should cause us to walk wisely, prayerfully, cautiously, but especially, unitedly. Jesus speaks in his John 17 prayer of two adversaries which are linked together – "the world" and "the evil one." In his gospel John uses the term "kosmos," translated "world" 57 times. Three times in his gospel, John uses the term – "Prince (or ruler) of this world" (12:31, 14:30, 16:11) to refer to "the evil one".

The "world" Jesus is praying about refers to the culture existing under the rulership of the evil one. Culture itself can be beautiful or destructive. Culture is not the enemy, but the enemy shapes culture then uses it as an enemy against the gospel. Culture under the evil one builds walls between people.

God loves unity in community. Since the devil hates what God loves, he seeks to divide and isolate. The Western "world" culture is especially laced with a poisonous thinking called "expressive individualism."

Five of the main tenets of this cultural disease are:

1. The highest good is individual freedom, happiness, self-definition, and self-expression.
2. Traditions, religions, received wisdom, regulations, and social ties that restrict individual freedom, happiness, self-definition, and self-expression must be reshaped, deconstructed, or destroyed.
3. The world will inevitably improve as the scope of individual freedom grows. Technology —in particular the internet—will motor this progression toward utopia.
4. The primary social ethic is tolerance of everyone's self-defined quest for individual freedom and self-expression. Any deviation from this ethic of tolerance is dangerous and must not be tolerated. Therefore, social justice is less about economic or class

inequality, and more about issues of equality relating to individual identity, self-expression, and personal autonomy.
5. Humans are inherently good.[11]

However, Jesus taught:

1. The highest good was not to be served but to serve.
2. Being united in the body of Christ where each member belongs to the other members is the path to personal fulfillment.
3. The world will improve the more the individual submits themselves to Christ and works together for God's mission.
4. Truth in love is the primary social ethic and sin must be repented of since it destroys both individual and community.
5. Humans are fallen and in need of transformation by the renewing of their minds.

This philosophy touting "expressive individualism" works directly against the need of community which God instilled in every human heart. Since God is a community and we are in his image, we are fulfilled and express God's goodness most effectively by living in healthy community.

But the evil one and world seek to destroy this value by sowing seeds of division wherever possible. Jesus had watched this happen in his own small band of disciples. John and James had come to him and said, "We want to sit on your right and left hand in glory." They made it about themselves rather than the team. The team did not respond well when they found out. Mark 10:41 tells us, "When the ten heard about this, they became indignant with James and John." Division had struck through the deceptive power of individualism.

This individualism comes dressed in many garbs - the racial segregation of the church, the celebrity culture in Christianity, the anonymous consumers that fill our larger churches, the dearth of accountability present in Christian growth, etc. This kind of individualism keeps the church from the unity Jesus was praying for. We must constantly be seeking protection from this kind of attack.

THE COUNTERCULTURE POWER OF CHRISTIAN COMMUNITY

I recall watching a documentary on how wolves will hunt down an elk. As long as the individual elk stay tight with the herd, they are safe. However, if an elk begins to separate itself from the herd, grazing in isolation, it often becomes the target of the wolves and invariably ends up as wolf food.

Jesus' prayer for protection probably caused the disciples to think back to his words in Luke 10:3 when he commissioned them "Go! I am sending you out like lambs among wolves." Sheep were created to flock together not to graze alone. Jesus sent them out two by two because community creates increased safety when ministering in wolf territory.

This is a key reason Jesus prays for our unity because he understands the dangerous realm we are living in. It is why one of the devil's primary strategy is division.

We must also realize the world will hate us because we often confront what our fallen culture loves. In our love for those in the world, we tell them God's truth. We shouldn't be surprised then when the world attacks us, but we must be prepared. This reality requires unity.

If you have ever sent a child off to the military during a time of war, or off to a secular college, you have had a feeling similar to the one Jesus has in this moment. They are marching into an atmosphere where they will be hated because of who they love and what they believe. Your general prayer is for their protection, but one of your specific prayers is that they would find others Jesus-followers who they could walk with, as they walk through the world's minefield.

One of the reasons the church has thrived under persecution is because oppression has pressed the church together. It has pushed secondary issues of doctrine and issues of ecclesiastical pride, down the ladder of priority so that churches begin to work together for the gospel.

There is an ancient Ethiopian proverb that says, "When spiders unite, they can tie down a lion." As 1 Peter 5:8,9 tells us we have power over the lion as we unite with the family of believers.

As my uncle in Africa said, "We will be safe from the lion, if we walk together."

CHAPTER TAKEAWAYS:

- Jesus taught us to resist our spiritual enemies daily.
- The Devil works through culture to divide people from one another.
- Christian Community is the effective defense against the devil's strategies.

CHAPTER 6

Together through Sanctification

17:14 *"I have given them your word and the world has hated them, for they are not of the world any more than I am of the world."*

17:16 *"They are not of the world, even as I am not of it."*

17:17 *"Sanctify them by the truth; your word is truth."*

17:19 *"For them I sanctify myself, that they too may be truly sanctified."*

"Tell me not of your justification, unless you have also some marks of sanctification. Boast not of Christ's work for you, unless you can show us the Spirit's work in you."

– J. C. Ryle

BIG IDEA: Ongoing sanctification is key to increasing unity with other believers.

EXPERIENCING TRUE SANCTIFICATION

Jesus prays "unify" in the same breath as "sanctify." Sanctification and unification of the church cannot be separated. To be unified as followers of Jesus, we must be separated from the world.

Growing up in a "holiness" church in rural Kansas, I heard the word "sanctification" many times. I couldn't define it, but I could describe it. It meant "no!" No alcohol, no smoking, no chewing tobacco, no movies, no swear words, no dancing and no cards (except "Rook" which was our church's form of poker). Sanctification seemingly had nothing to do with nurturing your marriage, serving the poor, speaking kindly at the beauty shop, helping the migrant workers, reaching out to the people of color, eating without gorging (gasp at the thought of fasting), or seeking unity with other Christians from the ten other churches in our town.

In fact, most of the other Christian churches in town were filled with "carnal" Christians. Those who drank alcohol, or smoked cigars, or watched "R" rated movies, weren't really fully Christians in our "holy" opinion. So when the "Fifth Sunday, all churches hymn sing" came around we always had to find out which church was hosting it to see whether we were participating. I was confused about how "sanctify" and "unify" fit together.

When Jesus starts his John 17 prayer, he thanks his Father that he has given eternal life to those who know him (17:2,3). But now his plea is that they would be "sanctified." "Not of the world" and "sanctify them by the truth" are closely linked in Jesus' prayer.

When Jesus is saying in his prayer that "he is not of this world," he is referring to what he repeatedly told his disciples – he had come from above (John 3:34, 8;23). Not only this, he had "sanctified" himself (John 17:19), separating himself from the desires, attitudes, values, motivations and idols of the world.

For the disciples to be "not of the world" meant that they too would come from above, not in the sense that Jesus did, but in being "born from above" (John 3:3). Regeneration is so dramatic, radical and pivotal that it can only be described as a "new birth." Every other metaphor falls short of describing this passing from death into life.

Since our identity is dramatically different than non-Christians (in that they have only been "born from below"), our desires and habits must be transformed to match our true identity.

"Not of the world" also meant the disciple's lives would stop being "conformed to this world" (Romans 12:2) and instead develop different cravings and be animated by a spiritual power (Acts 1:8). They would not create and live a long list of religious rules, but they would weigh everything on the scale of God's love for them and for others. This would lead them to say "no" and separate themselves from much of what the world loves. As Titus says, "For the grace of God has appeared that offers salvation to all people. It teaches us to say "No" to ungodliness and worldly passions, and to live self-controlled, upright and godly lives in this present age" (Titus 2:11-12).

But it would also inspire them to say "Yes" to what the world was saying "No" to - like the poor, the lepers, the widows, the rejected, the immigrants, the diseased, the imprisoned, the slaves, the minorities and sexual purity, generosity, honesty and humility. This would be why the world would hate them and call them "Jesus freaks." Their value systems were flipped from the culture around them. While the world walked by sight, they would walk by faith. As the world drew their "truth" from their own opinions , they would live and die for God's truth. To use the King James language, sanctified followers would be "peculiar" people (Titus 2:14, 1 Peter 2:9).

Sanctification is that process of becoming "less of this world" which will make us both a rebuke and an invitation to those living in this world. One of my college professors used to say, "Live so your life demands an explanation." Sanctification increases the need for an explanation. To the world, that can be something repulsive or attractive, something to persecute or something to explore. People tend to be like cockroaches, hiding from the light or like moths, drawn to the light.

THE TWO KINGDOMS AND THEIR CONSEQUENCES

Sanctification is about choosing kings and kingdoms. A few hours after Jesus prays, "Sanctify them by your truth," Jesus tells Pilate, "My kingdom is not of this world." Jesus draws the contrast between Pilate's "of this world" kingdom and his "not of this world" kingdom.

Jesus' John 17 prayer identifies these two kingdoms and he prays his followers would be delivered from the world and be deepened in the truth. Jesus had already taught his disciples the simple prayer of sanctification – "Thy kingdom come; thy will be done." This is the daily prayer that must be lifted up as an urgent plea, then lived in earnest determination.

Sanctification is a deeper listening and obedience to King Jesus' truth. His word becomes our command. His truth transforms our thinking. His revelation reveals our heart and motivations. His communication to us is Spirit and life (John 6:63). Our affection for and submission to his word makes us radically different than the world around us.

One of my ongoing prayers revolves around this intersection of my sanctification and His truth. Here's my prayer – "Lord, tell me the truth about me." I don't just want to know the truth; I want the truth to make me known to myself. "Expose all the places in my heart that are out of alignment with your will for me. Sanctify me by your truth."

Remember just before Jesus started praying in John 17, he had promised his disciples that the Spirit of truth would come and be a guide into all the truth (John 16:13). This "guiding" leads us not only further into the land of God's truth, but deeper into the territory of our own heart. His word is a searchlight shining into the dark corners of the closets of our lives to expose the truth about us. This disclosure is not for condemnation but for the liberation of sanctification.

SANCTIFICATION IS ESSENTIALLY MISSIONAL

Sanctification is missional. Sanctification has two sides – one is "set apart from" as in "set apart FROM the world;" the second is "set apart for" as in "set apart FOR the world." In Jesus' prayer, his plea for sanctification is immediately followed by the words, "As you sent me into the world, I have sent them into the world" (John 17:18). Jesus is praying that they will be different FROM the world FOR the sake of the world; that they will be holy so they can serve the world; that they will be changed so they can be world changers.

Personal transformation should always carry with it some missional motivation.

His kingdom coming more fully in my life means I am more useful in bringing his kingdom into the lives of those around me. I engage deeply with the world without catching its disease.

Sanctification is the only means of being in the world without becoming like the world.

The long-time preacher's analogy of the boat and the water is useful here. As Christians we are lifeguards on a rescue mission to save drowning people in an ocean of sin. Some Christians refuse to put their rescue rowboats into the water lest the water get inside the boat. Thus, they stand on shore yelling to the drowning, "Swim to us, come to us, there is safety on shore!" Not helpful.

Others put their boats into the water of the world thinking they will reach the lost by getting near them. However, the water looks cool, refreshing and fun, thus they begin to splash the water into the boat, until the boat begins to sink. Not helpful.

But there are a few others who launch their boats with a passion for the drowning, who come close to the perishing, who at the same time are diligent to keep the water out of the boat. These few rescue many. The moral of the story is essential: The boat must be in the water, but the water must not be in the boat.

The more we are sanctified, the more we will be unified. Jesus prays for the Father to sanctify his followers but then goes on to request that the believers may be made one (17:21). There is a direct connect here that we must not miss. We cannot say we are being sanctified if we are not being unified, AND being unified will not happen unless we continue to be sanctified. They serve each other.

CHAPTER TAKEAWAYS:

- Sanctification must be understood and pursued by every true Christian.
- More fully submitting to Jesus as King is an essential path towards togetherness.
- Sanctification is a necessity to more effectively reaching the world with God's love.

CHAPTER 7

Together in Mission

*17:18 "As you sent me into the world, I
have sent them into the world."*

*17:21 " . . . that all of them may be one, Father, just as
you are in me and I am in you. May they also be in us
so that the world may believe that you have sent me."*

*17:23b "Then the world will know that you sent me
and have loved them even as you have loved me."*

*17:25 "Righteous Father, though the world does not know
you, I know you, and they know that you have sent me."*

*"The Great Commission is too big for anyone to accomplish
alone and too important not to try to do together."*

– Steve Moore

BIG IDEA: Living on the Jesus mission demands working
in unity with other disciples.

SENT IN THE SAME WAY AS JESUS

When I read Jesus' prayer for us in John 17, I am struck by the fact
that the one sent from God was sending his friends for God. Jesus
was the "sent one" willing to receive a commission that knowingly
would require his own death. His earthly identity was grounded in

the commission his Father had given him. He had come to earth willingly but also at the will of His Father.

A surprising four times in his John 17 prayer, Jesus points out that he is the "sent one." He also declares that he is the sender (17:18). This "sentness" of Jesus is vital to understanding of who he is and who we are to be in him. That link is distinguished by this big two-letter word – "As" – meaning "in the same way the Father sent me into the world, I am sending you into the world." Jesus states this in his prayer here. But also four days later on the evening of his resurrection, Jesus shows up and pronounces it even more clearly. " . . . As the Father has sent me, I am sending you" (John 20:21).

Understanding HOW Jesus was sent gives us vital insight into how we are sent. How was Jesus sent? We could answer in various ways but for the purpose of this chapter we want to focus on two aspects. The first is that Jesus was "sent in order to send," or to expand the concept, "to make disciples who would go and make disciples." The second is that Jesus was sent to build a unified team. Our connection to one another cannot be separated from our connection with God.

THE JESUS MODEL FOR MISSIONAL IMPACT

We see the manner in which Jesus was sent by studying how he structured and carried out his ministry. The first ministry activity Jesus embarked on was to pray, select, and bring together a group of followers or disciples. The first call Jesus made to these disciples as he launched his mission was, "Come, follow me . . . and I will send you out to fish for people" (Matthew 4:19). Then we watched Jesus spend more than 75% of his time with the disciples in training them to carry out the mission themselves. His last words to them in Matthew's gospel were to go and replicate with others the same process he had done with them (Matthew 28:19,20).

In Jesus' last recorded words, we see this "sending" come to a poignant and powerful culmination - "But you will receive power when the Holy Spirit comes on you; and you will be my witnesses in Jerusalem, and in all Judea and Samaria, and to the ends of the earth" (Acts 1:8). Jesus was sending them to the ends of the earth just as he had been sent from heaven to earth. He was giving them the Spirit to empower them. He had also given them this model of being sent in order to select, disciple, equip and send others who would multiply the process.

Imagine there was a small group of people stranded on a deserted island, when suddenly a pile of building supplies fell from the sky, followed by a deep voice that sounded like Morgan Freeman saying, "Build a boat"." The people, however, were tired of living outside in the elements, so instead of constructing a boat, they built a house for them all to gather in and live more comfortably. They never escaped to freedom but lived and died in their small gathering place.

Jesus came and built a boat and trained 12 others to build boats. But somewhere along the way too many of his followers have become "house builders" instead of "boat builders." We have focused on building "gathering" places instead of "going" places. We have lived as consumers instead of disciple-makers. We have failed to live as "sent ones" like Jesus instructed and modeled.

In John 17 Jesus was praying we would use his model to reach the world. If we are to multiply the kingdom of Jesus, we must use the methods of Jesus. We must receive our "sending" and go forth, not to gather people around us and cling to them, but to send others out from us. We are sent to be senders. We are disciples who make disciple-makers.

UNITY IN DIVERSITY AS A SPIRITUAL TESTIMONY

But there are two other little words in Jesus prayer that are crucial for our mission. The words are "so that." Jesus prays, "that all of them may be one, Father, just as you are in me and I am in you. May they also be in us SO THAT the world may believe that you have sent me" (John 17:21). This a cause and effect statement. Becoming one will help win the world. Unity unleashes effectiveness. Credibility of the person of Jesus will be built by unity in the church.

The idea is so vital that Jesus repeats it in 17:23, "I in them and you in me--so that they may be brought to complete unity. Then the world will know that you sent me and have loved them even as you have loved me." As you read that verse, did you emphasize the word *then*? When? When the church is together, Jesus is revealed for who he really is. The more unified the church is, the more veracity Jesus' claim as Savior will have.

Collaboration allows a synergy that causes 1+1 to equal 3. "Two are better than one, because they have a good return for their labor" (Ecclesiastes 4:9). Unity empowers amazing amounts of evangelism to be done. But collaboration and unity also cause a testimony for the credibility of our message. Together we are significantly more believable than we are alone.

Jesus was sent to bring his diverse disciples together as a unified team. This is what Jesus prayed for – A supernatural unity brought on by the spiritual reality of being born again into the same family. Diverse people made one by the Son. A higher identity bringing people together by the common Spirit they share and the common cause they are committed to.

Jesus' disciples were a ragtag small group of extremely different kinds of men. Two were "sons of thunder" known for their temper, one was known for his impulsivity, another marked by skepticism and pessimism. There were fishermen, a government worker, probably a tradesman and a craftsman. One was a former Zealot with a passion to overthrow Roman rule while another was basically a traitor to the Jewish nation because he worked in collusion with Rome as a tax collector. The Zealot might have been happy to stick a knife in the tax collector's back, if the circumstances were right. Yet, these twelve became followers and worshippers of Jesus of Nazareth, spending three years traveling with him. They were a team. While they had their immaturities, disagreements and position-seeking, nevertheless, they were brought together by a common master. He chose dissimilar people to demonstrate the power of His love.

Now in this last prayer with his disciples before the cross Jesus prays that their unity would become the loudest testimony of his Messiahship. Jesus didn't want to use individuals, he wanted to use teams. He knew the mission would not be accomplished by gifted individuals but by common people working in unified teams. This would be a witness to the world but also a strategy to reach the world. Jesus chose a team of twelve, as well as others who traveled with him. Jesus taught the 72 who he sent out in teams of two (Luke 10:1). Paul always had partners and missionary teams with him in his work. The mission demanded spiritual and practical collaboration. This is why Jesus prays so earnestly for it.

There's a popular quote attributed as an ancient African proverb that says, "If you want to go fast, go alone. If you want to go far, go together." The American church has kept trying to "go fast." It has majored in addition instead of multiplication, in attraction rather than disciple-making, in platforming celebrities instead of equipping servants. Addition is faster than multiplication at first. But though coming together as teams of disciples who are "sent to become senders" is slower work, it will go infinitely further.

COLLABORATIVE DREAMS MORE THAN INDIVIDUALISTIC DREAMS

Paul summarizes this togetherness in his profound teaching on the nature of the church as a body. He writes, "As it is, there are many parts, but one body. The eye cannot say to the hand, 'I don't need you!' And the head cannot say to the feet, 'I don't need you!'" (1 Corinthians 12:20-21)

Our biggest and best dreams must be collaborative, not individualistic. We are not bodies, but body parts. We need one another to do the great things God has planned for us.

Our American individualism keeps lying to us saying, "You can do anything you want and be anything you want to be." This disconnects us, isolates us, causes us to dream of only what we personally can accomplish. The Spirit is saying, "You can be you and be the best body part ever, but you can't be the body part you aren't. So unite with the rest of the body, join with the whole church, and dream of what you can do together."

The scope of our mission demands the kind of unity Jesus prayed for. To bring the gospel to a culture living under spiritual deception demands the gifts of every disciple functioning together in an alternative community fueled by radical love. We need each other to accomplish the mission.

"Missionary Lesslie Newbigin noted that the whole church together communicates the gospel more powerfully than any individual Christian ever could. He called the church "the hermeneutic of the gospel" for the post-Christian West, by which he meant the church's life together should be a countercultural expression of the gospel's power and effects. In other words, the gospel produces communities of people whose corporate life is simultaneously offensive in its distinctness (1 Peter 4:3-4) yet winsome in its love for the world (Matt. 5:13–16).[12]

Will we be the answer to Jesus' prayer? We accomplish our gospel mission by blending our "togetherness" with our "sentness." We can't ignore the segregation of the church and divisions in the church while we merrily pursue our relationship with God and our mission for God. Jesus' prayer demonstrating our connection to God demands our connection with one another.

When God views our cities or towns, he ultimately sees one Church, not many. Each of the individual worshipping communities are various expressions of his one body in that city. Each church has gifts and resources which when brought together can take the mission of Christ much further. To reach a city for Christ will absolutely require a John 17 mindset.

We will be surprised who shows up when churches come together to live Jesus' John 17 prayer.

CHAPTER TAKEAWAYS:

- We are sent in the same way Jesus was . . . with his model and God's Spirit.
- Missional synergy only happens when we work in our giftedness together with other gifted disciples.
- Our unity in diversity is the truest testimony of Jesus' saving reality.

CHAPTER 8

Together through the Spirit

17:23 "I in them and you in me--so that they may be brought to complete unity. Then the world will know that you sent me and have loved them even as you have loved me . . . "

17:26 "I have made you known to them, and will continue to make you known in order that the love you have for me may be in them and that I myself may be in them."

"Spiritual life flows out of union with Christ, not merely imitation of Christ."

- Dr. Richard Lovelace

BIG IDEA: Jesus prayed that his indwelling presence would unify his followers.

THE INTERNAL TUNING FORK

In his book *The Pursuit of God*, author A.W. Tozer wrote the following:

"Has it ever occurred to you that one hundred pianos all tuned to the same fork are automatically tuned to each other? They are of one accord by being tuned, not to each other, but to another standard to which each one must individually bow. So one hundred worshipers [meeting] together, each one looking away to Christ, are in heart nearer to each other than they could possibly be, were they to become 'unity' conscious and turn their eyes away from God to strive for closer fellowship."[13]

For every true Christian, the tuning fork has taken up residence in their spirits. The decisive difference between Christians and non-Christians is the one who lives in them. "I in them" (John 17:26) are three of the most profound words Jesus could pray for us. "I in them" is the indwelling difference that makes the rest of the prayer possible.

"Who's in you" is the most important fact about you. This is the truth of Romans 8:9 – "You, however, are not in the realm of the flesh but are in the realm of the Spirit, if indeed the Spirit of God lives in you. And if anyone does not have the Spirit of Christ, they do not belong to Christ." One definition of a Christian is "a person in whom the Spirit of Christ lives."

"Who's in you" is also the most significant factor in coming together with those around you. Truly dwelling together depends on relying on the one who is indwelling us.

In John 17 Jesus prays that he might dwell in his disciples "so that they might be brought to complete unity" (John 17:23). This points out that our unity with one another is something that grows and develops toward "completeness." It also identifies the source of this growth as the indwelling Christ.

The Holy Mystic of Spiritual Unity

The unity Jesus was praying about must be understood as mystical, mystery and mastery. It is mystical in the sense that it is a brand of unity that rises far above our human existence and understanding. Jesus is praying about the kind of unity experienced within the Trinity itself. This spiritual unity is the kind of oneness Jesus experienced with the Father, both in heaven and in his incarnation.

Jesus prays, "I have given them the glory that you gave me, that they may be one as we are one—" (John 17:22).

Spiritual unity between believers is a divine and mystical work of the Spirit. We cannot manufacture it with willpower and emotional intelligence. It is far beyond cooperation and teamwork. It is not unity as in the United States or United Kingdom. It is not procured by creeds, councils, or church pronouncements. You cannot legislate or administrate the brand of unity Jesus prays for.

We may not fully comprehend this level of unity but we can believe for it, request it, prioritize it, and operate in its reality.

Have you ever had those moments in worship when something was happening that if you used secular language to describe it, you would call it "magical"? It went beyond the music, the words, the worship leader, the crowd, the lights. It felt like each individual voice had blended together into one voice of sincere and zealous praise. You may have had "Holy Ghost goosebumps" on your arms. You felt like you could hug every person in the room. If you've experienced something similar to this, you've had a taste of this mystical reality of the Spirit uniting his people in a moment of worship.

I am convinced the Spirit is working between believers in those ways on a continual basis -not in terms of emotional chills but in terms of spiritual realities. The indwelling Christ is actively engaging our spirits to be unified with the spirit of other believers. There is an inexplicable magnetic draw between the spirits of people who have Christ in them.

The Holy "Mystery" of Spiritual Unity

But the scriptures also describe this unity as a mystery. There was no deeper ethnic canyon between two ethnic groups than between the Jews and the Gentiles of Jesus' day. According to Barclay, "The basic sin of the ancient world was contempt. The Jews despised the Gentiles as worthless in the sight of God. At worst they existed only to be annihilated . . . At best they existed to be the slaves of Israel . . . ".[14]

Into this tense division came the great bridge builder who alone could connect both sides of the canyon - Jesus Christ. He and his followers were out to establish a new ethic of love based in the work of the cross and the message of grace flowing from it. Paul describes this as a "mystery" – "This mystery is that through the gospel the Gentiles are heirs together with Israel, members together of one body, and sharers together in the promise in Christ Jesus" (Ephesians 3:6).

Paul repeats this mystery of the gospel's work and connects it with the indwelling Christ – "To them God has chosen to make known among the Gentiles the glorious riches of this mystery, which is Christ in you, the hope of glory" (Colossians 1:26). It was the indwelling Christ who could bring believers together in the face of the worst prejudice ever. The mystery of the gospel's work is able to melt the icy hearts of hardened haters.

I have been in settings when ex-gang members who used to shoot one another on sight were now washing each other's cars and serving their community together because of their new life in Christ. I have been in Africa when warring tribes laid down their animosity and weapons due to becoming followers of the Lord of peace, Jesus Christ. I have watched divorced husbands and wives lay down their anger, hurt, and hatred due to the mystery of the gospel. I have stood with denominational leaders who once accused one another of blasphemy because of secondary doctrinal differences, reconcile and start working together for the gospel.

The Mastery of the Spirit to Make Us Peacemakers

This unity Jesus was praying for was not only mystical and mysterious, it was mastery. By mastery, I mean Jesus was praying his Spirit in his followers would become the master of their character, passions and efforts. Unity doesn't simply float on the spirit or arise from the gospel reality, it takes daily personal empowerment. Jesus called peacemakers the children of God but peacemaking takes daily effort.

Togetherness is built and sustained in atmospheres where the Holy Spirit has his way in the attitudes, words and actions of God's people. This is a moment by moment yieldedness to Spirit-directed responses to others. When Paul lists the fruit of the Spirit in Galatians 5:22, 23 he is giving us a primer in how to live in harmony as Christians.

It is instructive to see that in Galatians 5:19-21, Paul enumerates fifteen "acts of the flesh" and eight of them are directly pointed at separating us from one another. Hatred, discord, jealousy, fits of rage, selfish ambition, dissensions, factions and envy – each of these works powerfully against unity.

However, the fruit of the Spirit in Galatians 5:22, 23 operates just the opposite. All nine work together for unity. Love motivates you toward empathy. Joy is contagious. Peace makes you a peacemaker. Patience means you bear long and graciously with those who irritate you. Kindness looks for ways to express honor to those around you and thinks the best of others. Goodness is an integrity of life which makes you trustworthy to others. Faithfulness is a form of loyalty which deepens connections. Gentleness is a conscientiousness regarding how your words and actions will impact others. Self-control establishes discipline over your responses when offenses happen.

The fruit of the Spirit make you attractable and attachable. You attract people to yourself and to your church. Your life initiates unity. You build bridges. This priority for unity is one of the surest evidences of the fullness of the Spirit in a Christian's life.

The Spirit's expanding presence in our lives empowers us to do what is impossible on our own. The "indwelling" of Christ brings us a power to love our enemies and our brothers and sisters who sometimes act like enemies. It empowers us to forgive people in ways we would not on our own. It endows us with eyes to see past the behaviors into the heart of a brother or sister who is manifesting their pain in divisive ways.

My stepdad was a veterinarian who I helped treat dogs of all sizes. He always warned me, "Larry, be careful when you are holding dogs that are injured. You may be trying to help but dogs will usually bite whenever they are in pain." People are the same way. Don't be surprised and personalize it if they bite you. It is usually a sign they are in pain. As the old adage goes, "Hurt people hurt people". The Spirit will help us love people who are hurting, even if they bite. Christ is in them. Look for him under the pain.

William Barclay speaks of the indwelling of Christ in his followers: "Its (the church's) unity comes not from organization, or ritual, or liturgy; it comes from Christ. Ubi Christus, ibi ecclesia, Where Christ is, there is the Church. The Church will realize her unity only when she realizes that she does not exist to propagate the point of view of any body of men, but to provide a home where the Spirit of Christ can dwell and where all men who love Christ can meet in that Spirit.[15]

CHAPTER TAKEAWAYS:

- Christ's spirit in us is the means by which diverse disciples can become one in Christ.
- Christ's spirit works between believers in mystical ways that bring unity.
- Christ's spirit works through the mystery of the gospel to bridge the biggest gaps.
- Christ's spirit works through mastering our character so we become peacemakers.

CHAPTER 9
Together through Love

*17:23 "I in them and you in me—so that they may
be brought to complete unity. Then the world
will know that you sent me and have loved
them even as you have loved me. . . ."*

*17:26 "I have made you known to them, and will continue
to make you known in order that the love you have for
me may be in them and that I myself may be in them."*

*"Our love to God is measured by our everyday
fellowship with others and the love it displays."*
– Andrew Murray

*"The church is constituted as a new people who
have been gathered from the nations to remind the
world that we are in fact one people. Gathering,
therefore, is an eschatological act as it is the foretaste
of the unity of the communion of the saints."*
– Stanley Hauerwas

BIG IDEA: Jesus prayed that his love would increase in us
and between us to bring us together.

At the end of his life and ministry Jesus had one topic on the top
of his heart - LOVE. Not the generic brand of love which over
sentimentalized but the spiritual brand that is world-changing.

In 17:23, Jesus prays that his disciples would be unified as a witness to his identity *(the world will know that you sent me)* and also as a witness to the depth of his love *(and have loved them even as you have loved me)*. This is a staggering truth - the Father loves us in the same way he loved his Son.

RECEIVING THE FATHER'S UNEARNED LOVE

I can remember holding my newborn daughter for the first time in the delivery room. The miracle of a new human being sharing my DNA was stunning to me, but even more overwhelming was the love that I experienced for this little bundle of life. I felt my heart stretching and growing to accommodate the size of my love. Then it hit me, my dad who died when I was two years old, the dad I have not yet really seen, loved me that much.

Then I thought even further - "My Father God, whom I have not yet really seen, loves me as his son to that degree and beyond." Why? Why did I love my baby girl so much? Certainly not because of anything she had become or accomplished or given to me. But because she was mine. Not mine in a manner to own, control, or use for personal enhancement. But mine in that she came into being through Deb and me and she was my special assignment/privilege to love for a lifetime. For 35 years she has been a source of my greatest joys and deepest pains, but the love has not waned.

This is the essence of Jesus's statement in prayer in 17:23. We are loved by God in the same way Jesus was loved by his Father. Each individual daughter and son are so eminently valuable to his heart. Not because of our character, our win column, our intelligence, our discipline, our niceness, or our usefulness but because we are His.

My number one strength on the Strengthsfinder Test is "Achiever." I am wired to accomplish something every day. I feel more lovable if I have conquered a task or summitted a goal. It's tough to receive love "just because." It is disconcerting to be chosen just because I am me.

This is why I find the Father's words at Jesus' baptism so affirming. In Luke's gospel, before Jesus had performed one miracle, or preached one sermon, or trained one disciple, the Father makes an announcement. The words are for the bystanders but even more for Jesus. " . . . And a voice came from heaven: 'You are my Son, whom I love; with you I am well pleased;"(Luke 3:22). The Father expresses his love just because he is his Son.

Perhaps this occasion is in Jesus' mind and these words are ringing in Jesus' heart as he prays here in John 17. He pleads, "I want them to know you love them like you love me." This is a revolutionizing prayer we should pray for ourselves and for others - "Father, I want to know your love for me in the same way Jesus knew your love for him." Now that would be mind-blowing!

Receiving God's love individually is essential to the creation of unity. If we have to compete with others to earn love, they become a "frenemy". We act friendly but beneath the surface there is a rivalry hobbling unity. Also, insecurity of how we will be received causes a reservation in our freedom to express our love. Our comparisons block our connections. Insecurity undermines unity.

Insecurity creates a myriad of masks. We put on personas to be more acceptable to others. The result is gaps instead of connections, division instead of unity. Unity happens in the air of transparency. Authenticity is essential to love and paramount to unity.

FOLLOWING THE JESUS MODEL OF LOVE

Jesus is our love model. Living securely in the personal love of his Father, freed him to love people without hesitation, judgment, or comparison. The opinions of others were never his measuring tape. Therefore, their jeers didn't disrupt his love for them. Their cheers didn't cause his chest to swell nor lead to playing favorites. He never pretended to be someone he wasn't. Never tried to make himself a celebrity.

God is love. God is a community, a trinity to be precise. Therefore, God is the perfect expression of love in community. Father, Son, Spirit all expressing perfect love to one another which creates the consummate portrait of unity. Jesus was praying this picture into his disciples.

But Jesus was not simply painting a portrait to admire. The world tells us to paint a picture of loving our neighbor then hands us no paint. Jesus says, "Love the world," then says, "Study the picture of me doing it" AND "Here are the brushes and paints to do it with." He gives us all we need to paint towards the picture of unity we see in him. He is our source for love.

A simple, but profound revelation is found in 1 John 4:19 – "We love because he first loved us." Our love is only a derivative of His love. He loved us first and most and best. He keeps loving us and this love becomes the source of our love for others.

Most Christians falsely see themselves as pumps instead of pipes. Pumps have to bring the water to the surface through self-effort. Pipes simply receive the water from the source and channel it toward those who need it. The focus becomes staying fully open to receiving and giving more. We don't have to generate the water; therefore, we can flow without fear of running dry.

But we must hasten to declare the sacrificial nature of love lest it be construed as mere sentimentalism. This love Jesus was praying for his friends was the kind of love which would carry him to the cross the following day. It was not "Barney" kind of love comprised of big hugs, red hearts and happy faces. It was a prizing of the other person(s) to the degree that costly action would be taken on their behalf.

This is the daily call of the kind of love which leads to unity. It is action oriented, sacrificial, embodied, demonstrated love. In a word, it is the "cross." The cross defines what real love looks like – "This is how we know what love is: Jesus Christ laid down his life for us.

And we ought to lay down our lives for our brothers and sisters" (1 John 3:16).

A literal cross is not our daily reality but the message and power of the cross is.

Two of the most salient daily questions for disciples are "What ways have I sacrificed my rights and my time today to increase reconciliation in the world?" "How have I laid down a bit of my life today for my brothers and sisters?" Our manifest and tangible unity hinges on our answer to these questions of love.

LOVING THE TOUGH TO LOVE

There are people who are difficult to love, even (or should we say, especially) in the local or global church. Our challenge generally arises from the fact that we fail to agree with God about the person we suffer lack of love for. God values them far more than we do and sees infinitely more beauty in them than us.

It is impossible to detach love from mercy. Mercy is receiving or giving what is undeserved. Unity is not possible without love manifesting through mercy. Mercy grows tender hearts and tough skin. The tender heart is a sensitivity to the pain and predispositions of others; the acute awareness of refraining from unnecessary words or actions which would inflict pain. The tough skin is living in a default mode of forgiving hurtful words and actions before they penetrate our hearts and lodge there.

The mercy posture is what we might call the Porcupine Principle. On cold nights porcupines desire to huddle together to keep warm. However, as soon as they get close enough to help one another, they end up poking each other with their pointed quills. So they distance themselves again from one another, only to soon be suffering from the coldness of their isolation. The conundrum can only be solved by a combination of managing the quills and toughening the skin. Likewise for us, the answer is not to live at a cold, safe distance. It is to increase our mercy.

When the church in Rome was debating whether to eat meat offered to idols, did Paul tell them to start two churches - one for the meat-eaters and one for vegetarians? No. His solution was not separation but peace, acceptance, selflessness, love. Love must lead you together. If you are eating freely by faith but you aren't eating with sensitivity to your brother or sister's heart, you are missing the mark. Romans 14:15 says "If your brother or sister is distressed because of what you eat, you are no longer acting in love." Unity becomes the guiding ethic – "Let us therefore make every effort to do what leads to peace and to mutual edification" (Romans 14:19). "Each of us should please our neighbors for their good, to build them up" (Romans 15:2).

Since God is love, love is the atmosphere of heaven. Consequently, when Jesus taught us to pray that his kingdom would come on earth as it is in heaven, we are to continually ask God to establish his love as the atmosphere of our lives, our family, our churches and the entire body of Christ on earth. This is a key intersection between the Lord's prayer in Matthew 6 and the Lord's prayer in John 17. Leaders who understand the kingdom of God are praying for this spiritual yet tangible love to bridge divisions and saturate the church like an immersed sponge. Then as opportunities, challenges, disagreements and pressures squeeze the church, all that comes out is love.

CHAPTER TAKEAWAYS:

- Individually receiving the unearned love of God is essential to loving others well.
- Jesus is our pattern and power to love others.
- Loving those who are hard to love requires mercy and tenacity.

CHAPTER 10

Together in Our True Home

17:16 "They are not of the world, even as I am not of it."

*17:24 "Father, I want those you have given me
to be with me where I am, and to see my glory,
the glory you have given me because you
loved me before the creation of the world."*

*"We are in this life as it were in another man's house . . . .
In heaven is our home, in the world is our Inn: do not so
entertain thyself in the Inn of this world for a day as to have
thy mind withdrawn from longing after thy heavenly home."*

— Johann Gerhard

BIG IDEA: Keeping our true home in view helps us come together before we get there.

LOVING OUR TRUE HOME

We will soon be home together forever so we should walk together on the way. Our oneness in Christ is guided by the great reality of eternity together in the Father's house.

Where's "home" for you? Home has been identified as one of the strongest emotional words in the English language. Poverty is a stifling oppression, but homelessness is akin to hopelessness. When you lose your sense of place, your sense of belonging, you feel adrift in an infinite sea. There are no markers.

Home is where you are loved for who you are and feel most comfortable being you. Of course, a house is not a home. A house becomes a home when you feel safe there, when you can rest there, when you find joy and love there, when it's a place to recharge. For all but eight of our 40+ years of marriage, we have had teens who were not biological family living with us. With each new arrival we had one goal - to instill a sense of "home."

In John 17 when Jesus prays, "I want those you have given me to be with me where I am" (17:24) he is saying, "I want you to bring my family home." Jesus has just prayed twice that his friends were "not of this world" – meaning their home was somewhere else. They were only traveling ambassadors of the true kingdom to which they belonged.

Home for them was where their king reigns in uncontested glory, where their friend sits down to feast without persecution, where their Lord is recognized for who he really is, where they can all be together with Jesus in uninterrupted joy.

Make no mistake, complete unity is going to be a reality. Why? Because Jesus' prayer is going to be answered. When Jesus, accompanied by his followers, returns to reveal himself as King of Kings to all inhabitants of the world - opinions are going to cease. All debates about any doctrine will be done. Any distrust, suspicion or division between brothers and sisters will have been swallowed up in his perfect love and our perfected knowledge (1 Corinthians 13:12). As Jesus requested in his prayer, we will see his full glory (John 17:24).

"A home after our earth life is done" is a profound disruptor of our human worldview. Living without this hope of heaven causes us to try and create our personal version of heaven on earth. This feeds a scarcity mentality that breeds competition between us. Although Christians believe in heaven, this doctrine frequently fails to deliver us from a "create our piece of heaven here" mentality. As such, we too easily end up elbowing others out of our way in this pursuit. We become like Wal-Mart shoppers at Black Friday sales.

BRINGING HEAVEN'S UNITY TO EARTH

In the Matthew 6 prayer Jesus taught to his disciples (the so-called Lord's Prayer), he starts off with an emphasis on heaven. The Father is identified as the one "which art in heaven." Then he teaches us to intercede that this kingdom of heaven where the will of the Father is done would actually be manifested here - "thy kingdom come, thy will be done on earth as it is in heaven."

Jesus' prayers get answered! His John 17 prayer will be fully answered when he arrives to establish his rulership on the new earth. We are going to heaven but heaven is also coming to us. A primary attribute of this kingdom reign will be wolves hanging out with lambs and little kids leading lions around like puppies (Isaiah 11:6). Where there was division there will be absolute peace and unity. This heavenly place is where Jesus prays his still quite roguish and conflictual friends will come to (17:24).

If this is the atmosphere of his kingdom currently in heaven and soon to come fully to earth, then when we pray for the kingdom to be manifested, it is a prayer for unity among God's family. What we pray for, we must also be willing to work for. Often God asks us to consider how we might become answers to what we are asking him to do. The practical pursuit of unity is clearly a kingdom assignment from God. How are you working for unity?

Many Christians want to say prayers for unity then press their garage door openers, flop in front of the TV and live a detached life, especially from those different than themselves. But if Jesus is Lord, his example does not give us that option. He didn't just pray for the kingdom to come, he brought the kingdom through the way he lived his life. Through his love for his enemies and for those far from God, he closed the gaps between races, genders, ages and classes.

The dire warning, "Don't be so heavenly minded that you are of no earthly good," certainly pertains to a few believers. But most believers are "so earthly minded they are of no heavenly good."

This is what C.S. Lewis was saying . . .

"If you read history, you will find that the Christians who did the most for the present world were just those who thought most of the next. The apostles themselves, who set on foot the conversion of the Roman Empire; the great men who built up the Middle Ages; the English evangelicals who abolished the slave trade, all left their mark on earth, precisely because their minds were occupied with heaven. It is since Christians have largely ceased to think of the other world that they have become so ineffective in this." (Mere Christianity)

Being heavenly-minded is how you engage deeply in this world without becoming part of the fallen culture of this world. Your true home is so fixed in your heart, you just don't feel comfortable in this culture built on the dirt. This is much of what Jesus is praying when he says, "for they are not of the world any more than I am of the world." Their "minds are set on things above" (Colossians 3:2). They have little interest in building with "wood, hay or straw" (1 Corinthians 3:12). Give them eternal construction materials which will outlive them and which will go before them to heaven (1 Corinthians 3:13,14).

HOME IS WHERE TOGETHERNESS IS TREASURED

Home is where your loved ones are. You get this sense from Jesus as he prays, "I want them to be WITH me" (17:24). Remember when Jesus was choosing his disciples? I have often been moved by the motivation Mark records for Jesus' selection of the 12 disciples – "He appointed 12 that they might be WITH him and that he might send them out to preach" (Mark 3:14). Their companionship, friendship and unity with him was a major reason Jesus chose to have 12 friends. Should we be surprised then that Jesus gets to the time of his departure and prays, "Father, I want to be reunited soon and forever with my friends?"

There's an old gospel song that talks about a land that is wondrously fair with streets of gold and walls of jasper. But then the chorus grabs the heart of every true Christian – "Jesus will be what makes it heaven for me." Where Jesus is, is home for me.

Notice how Paul uses the word "home" in conjunction with "faith" - "For we live by faith, not by sight. We are confident, I say, and would prefer to be away from the body and at home with the Lord" (2 Corinthians 5:7-8). Our faith sees "home" and builds a preference to being there "with the Lord." Home is where he is and as long as we are here in the body, we will not be all the way home yet.

Our idea of "home" is one of the strongest unifying concepts we could lean into. There is one home and that is where Jesus is. In some glorious manner, which involves living beyond the space and time realities we currently are limited by, Jesus will be able to be personal with each one of us. We will be "gathered around his throne" in one place, in one spirit, singing one song, worshipping one Lord. Someone has cheekily said, "You will know it is heaven when all the Christians are agreeing on the same song to sing to Jesus." But we will be there in perfect unity to honor the Lamb who was slain.

Revelation 5:9 - "And they sang a new song, saying: "You are worthy to take the scroll and to open its seals, because you were slain, and with your blood you purchased for God persons from every tribe and language and people and nation.""

It is staggering to think that the divisions of tribe, tongue, ethnicities, nationality (and we might as accurately include denomination, political party, economic class, gender, generation, selfish ambition, etc.) are all obliterated. We will each still be distinct - gloriously connected to our earthly identity - yet, having been spiritually united in a way that distinctions blend together as in a vivid rainbow. In a rainbow each color is discernible, though not distinct so as to be elevated, but rather to serve the overall beauty and mission of the rainbow.

Since we are all the same family, saved by the same Savior, headed for the same home forever, THEN why not lock arms with one another now? If Christ is in you and Christ is in me and Christ desires to be WITH both of us, then we must let Christ bring us together now. We must hurdle any obstacle that hinders our unity. We can't be "with Christ" without being "with those we disagree with" who also know Christ.

My home growing up in rural Kansas was one of those big farmhouses with lots of space for plenty of people. We had three refrigerators and two freezers always full of an array of food. The alluring aroma of freshly baked pies and cookies usually filled the air. In our basement was a room with seven comfy beds. Gospel music played almost continually. The house had an ambiance of acceptance and love. My mother was always inviting someone or some group to spend the night – the African-American gospel quartet, the migrant workers, the pheasant hunters, the visiting minister, my sister's college friends, the town drunk, etc.

Often times the dinner table had lively discussions where people disagreed earnestly with one another . . . but it was hard to have bad attitudes with your mouth full of pumpkin pie. Many times mom would sit down at the piano and begin to play some hymns. If you knew the song you sang, if you didn't you hummed along.

But to me what truly made our house a true home was the fact that "Jesus was there." He was honored at every meal and the Bible was either on or beside the table. His presence brought people together in a unique way, even if they were without faith in him.

I know what I experienced was rare and is now antiquated in many ways. But the longing for home is as current as your heart today. This hunger is built into us. Jesus' great prayer captures his desire for us as well. To be together as one is his yearning and ours.

While such a home is still ahead, we can enjoy important foretastes of it here if we will pursue what Jesus prays for us in John 17. As we head "home" we can call out to those traveling the wrong way. Many of them will do U-turns and come with us, for home is what every person really wants.

CHAPTER TAKEAWAYS:

- The reality of our forever home has strong implications for how live now.
- Bringing heaven to earth is a call to bring heaven's unity to earth's divisions.
- Togetherness will be a defining characteristic of our true home.

CONCLUSION

"The grace of the Lord Jesus be with God's people. Amen."
Revelation 22:21

*"Amen is not the end of a prayer, it just gets
us ready to go to the next level."*
– Gary Busey

Was the last word of Jesus' prayer, "Amen"? *Amen* is not recorded
at the end of John 17, although it is likely Jesus said it. Jesus would
likely seal such a pivotal prayer with this declaration – "Amen! - may
it be fulfilled." Jesus announced "Amen" over 70 times in scripture.

Amen is the last word in our Bible.

Henry Morris states, "The word "amen" is a most remarkable
word. It was transliterated directly from the Hebrew into the Greek
of the New Testament, then into Latin and into English and many
other languages, so that it is practically a universal word. It has
been called the best known word in human speech. The word is
directly related — in fact, almost identical — to the Hebrew word
for "believe" (amam), or faithful. Thus, it came to mean "sure" or
"truly," an expression of absolute trust and confidence."[16]

Amen is a unifying word. It brings people together. It declares
a oneness. It binds them together. It blesses them. It commissions
them!

If Jesus concluded his prayer with "Amen," it is likely the
disciples responded in unison, "Amen!" Jesus was saying, "may it be

fulfilled" and the disciples were saying "truly!" We have something similar in the diverse church I serve. When I make an important point in my message, I state a question for emphasis – "Amen?!" and with one voice they reply back, "Amen!". We are saying, "That's the truth!" or "I agree" or "That's for sure!" We collaborate to say the amen and cement the truth in ourselves and each other.

The church needs to learn a stronger, "Amen!" to God and one another.

What Jesus has prayed for us can be trusted and relied upon! Amen? Amen!

We can enjoy a more profound spiritual union with God! Amen? Amen!

The unity Jesus prayed for us can be lived out in spiritual and practical ways! Amen? Amen!

Living Jesus' greatest prayer will require us to . . .

1. develop ever-deepening lives of PRAYER
2. give God the GLORY he deserves
3. invite the TRUTH to shape our hearts, minds and hands
4. live in the power and exaltation of the one NAME of Jesus
5. actively resist the deceptions and attacks of the EVIL ONE
6. surrender to the ongoing SANCTIFICATION of the Spirit in our lives
7. passionately live on the only MISSION worthy of our lives
8. rely moment by moment on the indwelling presence of the SPIRIT of Christ
9. pursue LOVE as the first and greatest gift and treasure
10. yearn for HOME while offering a taste of home to others along the way . . .

Above all it will require us to live together with God and with our sisters and brothers. Amen? Amen!

A MODEL PRAYER

Praying the Essence of John 17

*Father we come to you in the amazing grace of **prayer**.*
We come believing you hear and respond to our prayers.
*We seek to **glorify Jesus** through our lives and ministries and*
*to see more of the **glory** of **Jesus** in our brothers and sisters.*
*Bring us together as one people for your **glory**.*
*Thank you for the **truth** of your Word,*
May we live by its truth and be unified by its power.
*Thank you for being **Jesus**, our Savior.*
*Help us to live only for your **name** and not our own.*
*We know the **evil one** wars against us, so please*
*protect us by the power of your **name**.*
*Please **sanctify** us from the sin of the world*
and for the sake of the world.
*Impassion us for the **mission** you have sent us on,*
*Empower us by your **Spirit** for this **mission**.*
*Unify us by your **Spirit** so the world will see who you really are.*
*May your **love** be the defining characteristic*
of our lives and of every relationship.
*Please help us live for our true **home** and not our temporary one.*
We look forward to being with you
and with one another for eternity.
Amen

ABOUT THE AUTHOR

Larry serves as the Lead Pastor of Light & Life Christian Fellowship in Long Beach, CA. Starting with a handful of committed "white folks," the church has grown into a large multi-ethnic church transforming its tough urban neighborhood. A priority on local and global church planting has led to the start of 19 churches nationally and dozens in Ethiopia, Philippines and Indonesia.

Larry also oversees the church planting efforts of his denomination in Southern California where they are planting 50 new churches in 5 years. Holding a doctorate in church leadership and as the author of six books, Larry speaks and consults frequently. Azusa Pacific University has recognized Larry with the Centennial Award naming him one of the most influential graduates in its history. Larry serves on the Board of Trustees for Azusa Pacific University. Larry also serves as the Director of Spiritual Engagement at Exponential.

Larry and Dr. Deb Walkemeyer have been married for 38 years. They have two adult daughters. Larry enjoys snow skiing, waterskiing, biking, traveling, mission trips with 20-somethings and long walks on the beach.

NOTES

1. https://www.google.com/search?q=define%3A+collaborate&o-q=define%3A+collaborate&aqs=chrome..69i57j69i58.6423j1j7&-sourceid=chrome&ie=UTF-8, accessed September 22, 2019.

2. https://africa.thegospelcoalition.org/article/redeeming-ubuntu/

3. http://www.cslewisinstitute.org/webfm_send/577, Revival Born in a Prayer Meeting, accessed August 18, 2019

4. https://www.ministrymatters.com/all/entry/5525/wesley-a-man-of-one-book-and-a-thousand, accessed August 22, 2019.

5. https://thinktheology.co.uk/blog/article/primary_and_secondary_issues_how_do_we_tell_the_difference, accessed September 22, 2019.

6. https://www.ligonier.org/learn/articles/essentials-unity-non-essentials-liberty-all-things/, accessed August 22, 2019.

7. https://www.christianitytoday.com/news/2019/august/efca-drops-premillennialism-evangelical-free-church-teds.html, accessed August 25, 2019.

8. http://www.drurywriting.com/keith/faith.meltdown.story.htm, accessed August 22, 2019.

9. https://en.wikipedia.org/wiki/Agree_to_disagree accessed Dec 29, 2019.

10. https://www.thegospelcoalition.org/blogs/kevin-deyoung/5932/, accessed August 24, 2019

11. https://www.thegospelcoalition.org/blogs/trevin-wax/expressive-individualism-what-is-it/

12. https://www.christianitytoday.com/edstetzer/2019/august/what-missionaries-can-teach-us-in-post-christian-america.html

13. https://ministry127.com/resources/illustration/tuned-to-christ, accessed September 14, 2019.

14. https://www.studylight.org/commentaries/dsb/ephesians-3.html, accessed September 14, 2019.

15. https://www.studylight.org/commentaries/dsb/ephesians-2.html, accessed September 14, 2019.

16. https://www.icr.org/article/amen/

Made in the USA
Middletown, DE
22 July 2020